INCREDIBLY DISGUSTING DRUGS

COCAINE AND YOUR NOSE
The Incredibly Disgusting Story

Melanie Ann Apel

the rosen publishing group's
rosen central
new york

Published in 2000 by The Rosen Publishing Group, Inc.
29 East 21st Street, New York, NY 10010

First Edition

Apel, Melanie Ann.
    Cocaine and your nose : the incredibly disgusting story / Melanie
    Ann Apel.
       p.   cm. — (Incredibly disgusting drugs)
    Includes bibliographical references and index.
    Summary: Explains the parts and functions of the nose, how the body breathes and smells, the effects of the drug cocaine, and how to get treatment for addiction.
    ISBN 0-8239-3251-6 (lib. bdg.)
    1. Cocaine—Toxicology—Juvenile literature. 2. Nose—Juvenile litera-ture. 3. Respiratory organs—Juvenile literature. [1. Cocaine. 2. Drug abuse. 3. Nose. 4. Respiratory system.] I. Title. II. Series.
    RA1242.C75 A64 2000
    616.86'47—dc21   00-020210

Manufactured in the United States of America

CONTENTS

Introduction: Get On Board!   4

1   Anatomy of a Nose   6

2   The Respiratory and
        Olfactory Systems   12

3   The Real Deal on Cocaine   19

4   Cocaine, Your Nose, and
        the Rest of Your Body   30

5   Keeping Clean   42

Glossary   44
For More Information   45
For Further Reading   46
Index   47

Introduction: Get On Board!

Hold on to your hats because you're about to go on a wild ride through the human body. Along the way, you'll see some pretty gross pictures; learn some interesting, important, and maybe even life-saving facts; and find out exactly what happens to your body—on the outside and the inside—when you take cocaine.

Today about 5 million Americans use cocaine. Although the total number of cocaine users in the United States has gone down by 75 percent since the mid-1960s, more and more young people are trying this drug. In fact, according to a 1998 study, more than half of the Americans who had used cocaine during one month were young adults. That comes out to more than 700,000 teenagers doing some pretty dangerous drugs—drugs that can kill you, even if you only use them once.

Infarction, or blockage in blood circulation, of the human lung is often caused by drug abuse. The areas in red represent damage to the blood cells and lining of the lung. In a healthy lung, these areas would be clear.

Wait . . . so cocaine can kill you the first time you use it? That's right. Anyone—including young, healthy first-time users and even highly trained athletes—can die from just one use. And it doesn't matter how much cocaine you use. Even a small amount can cause heart attacks, really high fevers, strokes (not enough oxygen in the brain), and convulsions (very violent shaking), all of which can lead to death.

Some other common effects of cocaine are blurry vision, breathing problems, headaches, damage to the brain and lungs, and coughing up blood. Sounds awful, doesn't it? We haven't even looked at all the bad stuff that cocaine can do to your nose. The fact is, cocaine is a killer. Your nose is only the beginning when it comes to the damage cocaine can cause. So don't touch that dial. Stay tuned for an up-close look at the incredibly disgusting effects of cocaine—not just on your nose, but on your entire body.

1 Anatomy of A Nose

Your body needs oxygen to live. To get this oxygen, your body uses a process called respiration. Your lungs take in oxygen and pass it to your blood. Your blood then carries the oxygen all over your body, delivering it to your body's tissues and organs. Your lungs also get rid of carbon dioxide, the stale, used air in your body.

Your nose (along with your mouth) is the starting point of the respiratory system. In addition to bringing in fresh oxygen, your nose is responsible for keeping dust and dirt from getting into your body and for warming and humidifying (moistening) the air you breathe in.

Interior Nose Diagram

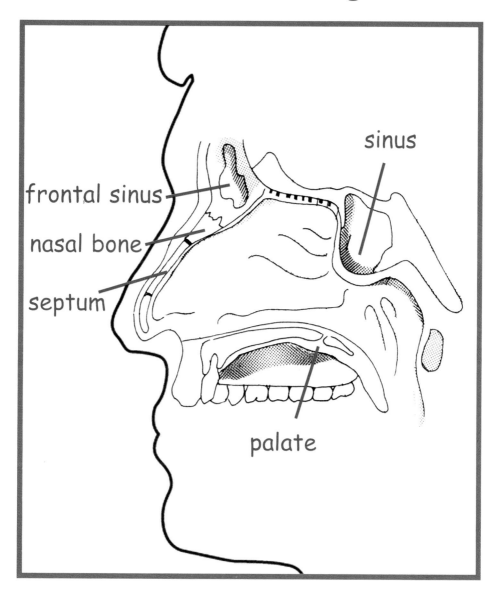

sinus

frontal sinus

nasal bone

septum

palate

Aside from being a main entrance to your respiratory system and trapping all that dirt and dust, your nose has another important job. It is the main sense organ involved in smelling. By sniffing out millions of smells around you, your nose gives you very important information about your surroundings. Your nose smells smoke and lets you know that you should escape from a burning house. It tells you that possibly harmful chemicals, like model glue or turpentine, are nearby. The smell of eggs and pancakes can be your wake-up call to breakfast on a lazy Saturday morning. How does your little nose do such an important job, you ask? Keep reading.

THE INS AND OUTS

Let's explore the human nose more closely. Obviously, the outside of your nose is a lot easier to examine than the inside, so let's start with that.

Along with your mouth, your nose is the main entry and exit for air to get to and from your lungs. It is made of two main materials: bone, which is very hard and unbendable, and soft tissue, which is a combination of fat and skin. You will notice that the tip and sides of your nose are softer than the bridge—the long, straight part—of your nose. That's because these parts are made of that soft tissue.

The long, straight part of your nose is made of bone and something called cartilage, which is a special kind of soft tissue that is not as tough as bone but is much sturdier than regular soft tissue.

Exterior Nose Diagram

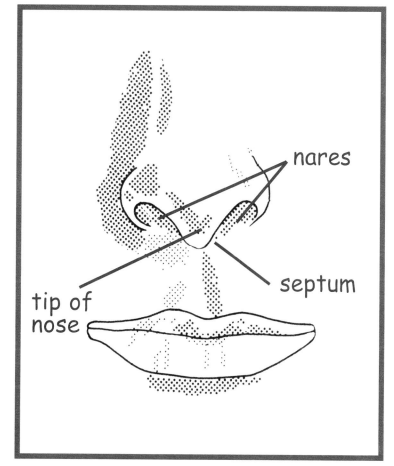

nares

septum

tip of nose

Looking at the lower part of your nose, you'll see two openings, one on each side. These openings, called nostrils, lead to the deeper, darker, not-so-easily-seen areas of your nose—the nares, or internal passages. The nares are separated by a piece of bone called the septum. The nares lead to the nasal cavity, a chamber (hole) directly behind your outer nose where the air you breathe in goes to get warm. On either side of the nasal cavity are smaller chambers called sinuses.

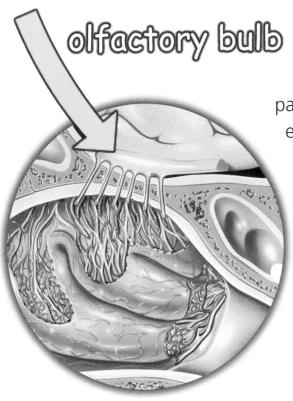

olfactory bulb

The brain's olfactory bulb allows for the detection and interpretation of different smells. Damage to olfactory nerve cells, a frequent result of cocaine use, can permanently destroy one's sense of smell.

The Mucus Membrane

The whole respiratory passageway—from the entrance to the nasal cavity down through your throat and into your lungs—is lined by a mucus membrane that has many special properties. One such property is the ability to sense smells around you and send information about these smells to the brain.

Tiny olfactory hairs on the roof and sides of the nasal cavity are responsible for detecting smells and sending the information to nerve cells on the top of the cavity. From there, the signals are sent to the olfactory bulb and then interpreted by your brain as different smells. (Check out chapter 2 for more details on smelling.)

Another responsibility of the mucus membrane is to detect germs and viruses in your body. When white blood cells in the membrane sense signs of an infection in your body, they call in your body's natural defenses to help get rid of the unwanted visitors.

What About the Throat?

Have you ever had the odd experience of taking a sip of milk or soda only to have it come shooting out of your nose? That's because your nose and mouth are connected by your pharynx (the scientific term for throat). Normally, when you drink, your body pushes the liquid down toward your stomach by swallowing. But if there is liquid in your throat that gets pushed upward instead (say, because you sneeze or start laughing really hard in the middle of drinking), the liquid can enter your nose. When that happens, it has nowhere to go but out through your nostrils!

2 The Respiratory and Olfactory Systems

As we saw in chapter 1, your nose, along with your mouth, is the starting point of a very important system in your body—the respiratory system. The respiratory system is the set of organs—including your nose, mouth, and lungs—that enable you to breathe. Air from outside your body gets into your body through your nose. Your nose then performs several very important functions on this air before it enters the rest of your body.

First of all, your nose is responsible for filtering out dirt, dust, pollen, germs, even tiny insects flying in the air—anything that could make you really sick if your nose weren't there to keep it from getting into your body. How does your nose do this?

There are two main ways that your nose filters the air around you. First, the hairs that line the inner passages of the nose form a barrier to keep out small particles. Your nose's second weapon against unwelcome intruders, believe it or not, is mucus—yep, that slimy stuff that comes out when you blow your nose. Dust, dirt, and other floating particles that we inhale get trapped by the sticky mucus and never get farther into the body. Then when we blow our noses, these particles get flushed out along with the mucus.

A second important job your nose performs is humidifying and warming the air it brings into your body. All this means is that your nose makes the air moist and warm before it goes into your body. If your nose didn't do this, breathing

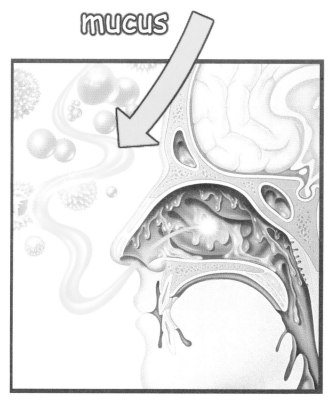

mucus

Mucus membranes moisten and protect the respiratory system, filtering dust, dirt, and germs from inhaled air. Cocaine use damages the mucus membranes, leaving the body vulnerable to viral and bacterial infections.

air in and out would be pretty uncomfortable because the cold, dry air would be a shock to your system.

Think about what it's like when your nose gets stuffed up from a cold. You have to do all your breathing through your mouth, right? Try this for a minute or two by holding your nose tightly. Is the inside of your mouth starting to feel dry? What about your throat? That's why having a healthy nose to breathe through is so important!

WHAT'S THAT SMELL?

The other job of your nose is to smell things. This has been mentioned already, but let's get into it a little more here. We all know that odors, or smells, come in many different varieties. Some odors, like the smell of Thanksgiving dinner or fresh flowers, are very nice to have around. Others, like your brother's feet, aren't quite as pleasant. Whether you are smelling nice odors or awful ones, your sense of smell is very important in keeping your body safe and healthy. Your sense of smell helps you get important information. For example, smelling a certain type of perfume may let you know that your favorite aunt is somewhere nearby. Sniffing a container of milk can tell you whether it's okay to drink or if you should trash it right away.

For one reason or another, some people don't have as

good a sense of smell as other people do. In addition to being a drag (imagine not being able to smell grape bubble gum or fresh brownies!), having a poor sense of smell can be a real problem. Think about what it would be like if you couldn't count on your nose to tell you important things, such as that the room you are in has been recently painted or that something is burning in the oven. You might end up with some fresh wet paint on your new shirt or, far worse, a house fire.

Super Sniffers

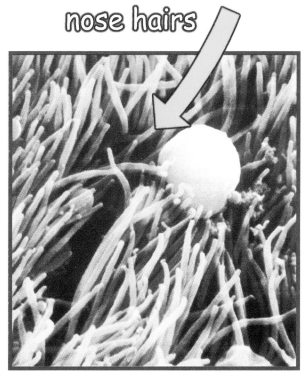

nose hairs

How does a healthy nose sniff out smells? It starts just after air is filtered by the nostrils and is on its way to the lungs through the nasal cavity (right behind your outer nose). On the roof and sides of the nasal cavity, there's a small area of nerve cells—only about the size of a postage stamp—that start off the smelling process.

Cilia, or tiny hairs inside the nasal cavity, allow for the transportation of fluids like mucus throughout the respiratory system.

HAAAA-CHOOO!

Why do you sneeze? When dirt or extra mucus enters your nose, it can irritate the linings of the air spaces inside your nose. This irritation makes you take a deep breath and then blast air through your nose at more than 100 miles (or 161 kilometers) per hour to get rid of the intruder!

If you look at one of these nerve cells under a microscope, you'll see millions of tiny hairlike structures, called cilia, along the edge of the cell. These cells are covered with receptors sensitive to odor particles in the air.

The receptors are your body's private detectives, always on the prowl for smell molecules lurking around your nasal passages. There are around 10 million receptors in your nose, and there are at least twenty different types of receptors. Each type can sense a different range of smell molecules. When one set of receptors senses the presence of smell molecules, those receptors send the information, in the form of nerve signals, along your olfactory (smell) nerve to your brain's smell center.

When new information comes in from the olfactory nerve, the smell center gets busy analyzing the signal pattern and identifying the smell. Based on the information gathered by the cilia and the olfactory nerve, plus what it already knows from past smelling experiences, your brain says "good smell" or "bad smell" and then tells you what the smell is.

Matching a smell to an object or person can happen almost immediately, but at other times your brain might need a few moments to figure out what you're smelling. Sometimes, of course, your brain doesn't recognize the smell at all, and you are left to guess what the smell is.

NOSE NEWS

Have you ever smelled something and immediately felt a strong emotion? The reason we associate smells with events or people is that the part of your brain that is responsible for smelling is also responsible for your emotions and your memory. This part of the brain is called the limbic system (hmmm, let's see—think you can remember that?).

limbic system

The brain's nerve pathways and thalamus, shown in red, allow for the reception of sensory information. These nerves lead into the brain's limbic system, shown in yellow. Damage to this system can interfere with one's ability to recognize pain and emotions.

3 The Real Deal on Cocaine

Okay, so we've seen that the nose has some pretty important responsibilities. We've also seen that the way it works is complicated. That means that when you snort cocaine, you could be damaging the system at many different levels. And that means trouble. Keep reading to learn the gory details about what cocaine can do to mess up this fragile system.

COCAINE AND YOUR BODY

When you think of having fun or having a good time, what kinds of activities come to mind? Do you think of watching a movie, going to a party, or hanging out with friends? Or do you prefer going to an amusement park, a football game, or the beach?

People use drugs for lots of different reasons, but one of the most common reasons, especially for young people, is that they think doing drugs is a way of having a good time. Even when kids know that drugs like cocaine can be really dangerous, they never think that those bad things could happen to them.

The problem is, they're wrong. Dead wrong, in fact. Drugs like cocaine can kill anyone, of any age, at any time. Thousands of kids and teens die every year just from trying out new drugs once "to see what it's like." Young people

with perfectly healthy hearts can die of a heart attack just from using cocaine one time. Cocaine can kill athletes who are in top shape by stopping their breathing.

Even if cocaine users don't die right away, they can suffer some pretty serious consequences from their drug use. According to one study, 31 percent of all people sent to emergency rooms in 1997 for health problems related to drug use had taken cocaine. No other drug even came close to causing the same number of emergencies (the runner-up, heroin, led to 14 percent of visits). And the problem isn't getting any better, especially when it comes to kids and teens. The same study reports that emergency room visits related to cocaine use increased by 77 percent between 1995 and 1997 among young people between the ages of twelve and seventeen.

COCAINE AND THE LAW

In addition to the extremely severe health problems that cocaine can cause, it can also lead to some serious problems with the law. That's because buying, selling, and using cocaine are all illegal.

Does getting caught by the police sound like fun? How about telling your parents that you've been using drugs? In some cases, you may even be sent to jail or be forced to do

community service if you are caught possessing cocaine. Although some teens and adults think that doing hard drugs like cocaine is "having a good time," they probably don't feel that way when they wind up in jail—in a cell like the one on the left!—or in the emergency room.

Even when people are aware of the damage that cocaine can cause, they never think that they will be the victim. "I knew that cocaine could kill you, but I never thought it would happen to someone I know," says Kim, fourteen. "Shana was only thirteen when she died, and it was her first time taking cocaine." Nobody is safe from the dangers of drugs.

WHAT IS A DRUG ANYWAY?

A drug is any substance you take—whether it is man-made or from a natural source—that changes the way you think, feel, or act. There are lots of different kinds of drugs that do many different things to your body, and there are lots of different ways to use these drugs.

All Drugs Are Not Alike

So far we've been talking about cocaine and other "hard" drugs, like heroin, that are illegal to use, sell, and buy. But there are plenty of legal drugs, too. Aspirin and cough medicine are examples of drugs that you can easily buy at the supermarket or drugstore without special permission.

A few drugs are legal for most people, but not everyone. In the United States, for example, there are minimum ages for buying and using alcohol and tobacco products (like cigarettes and chewing tobacco), which are considered drugs.

And then there are drugs that are legal to buy, sell, and use, but only when a doctor has prescribed them for you. Some common prescription drugs are medications for

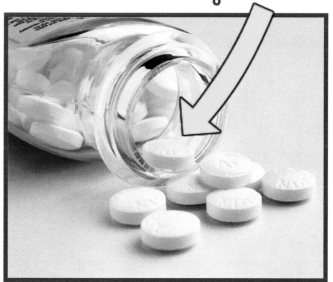

aspirin

asthma, antibiotics for infections, and painkillers for people who have just had an operation or who have a bad injury.

It's important to know that even though these kinds of drugs are legal, they can be just as dangerous as illegal drugs if they are not used the way they are meant to be used. All drugs can be harmful: legal drugs that are taken for too long or in too large a dose, medicines used without a prescription, and illegal drugs used to get high.

THE DIRT ON COCAINE

As you now know, cocaine is an illegal drug. It is also one of the most addictive substances known to man. This means that once you start using cocaine, it's really hard to stop.

Cocaine is in a category of drugs called stimulants. Other drugs in this category include amphetamines (also known as pep pills or uppers) and caffeine, which is found in coffee, tea, and chocolate. Strong stimulants like cocaine make your heart beat

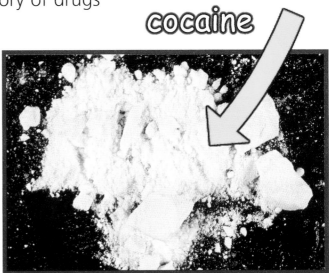

cocaine

really fast, sometimes so fast that it gets tired out and stops beating altogether. Stimulants can also make you really nervous and unable to concentrate.

Aside from physically damaging the body, cocaine can also ruin a person's life. Once someone is addicted—and that can happen after the first try—he or she will do anything to get more of the drug. Being addicted to a drug means that you need the drug just to get through each day. This can make you spend all of your money and then steal more; lose your home, job, and family; and go to jail.

Where Does Cocaine Come From?

Cocaine has been around for hundreds of years. Most of it is grown in South American countries like Bolivia and Peru. People who lived there a long time ago used to chew on the leaves of the coca plant because the leaves gave them the energy they needed to work high up in the mountains without much food. They also used the coca leaves in religious ceremonies.

For many years, Indians grew mainly vegetable crops and only small numbers of coca plants. Eventually illegal drug traffickers (people who buy and sell illegal drugs) made the Indians stop growing their healthy vegetable crops and grow only coca plants instead. Soon the Indians

The coca plant, or *Erythroxylon coca,* is the primary source of cocaine.

learned to mix coca leaves with kerosene and then dry the mixture in the sun to make a yellow paste. When smoked, this paste made the user feel very good. Today this paste is smoked not only by the Indians but by people all around the world.

Most of the paste made in Bolivia, Peru, and other nearby countries is sent to Colombia, another country in South America. Colombia is home to the people who control most of the cocaine traffic in the world. They are the ones who make the actual cocaine and then ship it to the United States and other parts of the world, where people use it to get high.

A little over 200 years ago, that same coca plant found its way to Europe. The first actual cocaine as we know it today was not made until 1855. At that time, cocaine was used as an anesthetic, a drug that makes the body numb and unable to feel pain. But even then, people knew that cocaine could cause pleasure, too. Some people were already taking cocaine for fun.

Since cocaine was cheap and easy to get back then, doctors began giving it to their patients to treat many different health problems. Cocaine was also added as an ingredient in many medicines because patients felt really good after taking it. Of course, what doctors didn't know back then was that this good feeling is only temporary and that cocaine use is actually extremely dangerous. They had no idea that there would be negative side effects to putting so many people on cocaine. As a result, many people ended up with far more serious problems, including addiction and death.

Do You Drink Coke?!

Here's a really weird factoid about cocaine: It was an ingredient in the first recipe for Coca-Cola. When Coca-Cola first came out in 1885, it was considered a healthy (!) drink because people felt energized and happy after drinking it. Believe it or not, Coca-Cola contained cocaine for the first twenty years that it was sold.

Cocaine was removed from the drink around 1905, when doctors finally realized that cocaine wasn't good for people. People were getting sick and even dying from taking too much cocaine, so doctors stopped prescribing it, too. Thanks to the Pure Food and Drug Act of 1906, any use of cocaine for nonmedical purposes was declared illegal.

WHO USES COCAINE AND WHY?

Even though cocaine has been basically illegal since 1906, people have continued to use it anyway. In the early days, cocaine was cheap and easy to get, but its price eventually went way up and people had to spend a lot more money to get it.

In the 1960s, people started using drugs much more often and in greater amounts than ever before. This is when the use of cocaine, as well as many other drugs, became popular again. People from all walks of life used cocaine: rich people and poor people; kids, teenagers, and adults; people with lots of education and others with very little schooling.

What all of these people have in common, however, is that they are at an extremely high risk of becoming addicted to cocaine, even after using it only once. An addiction isn't just mental (all in your head). It becomes physical, too, so that your body needs the drug in order to feel normal. John Belushi (the guy in the photo) was a famous comedian who was addicted to cocaine. He eventually died of a cocaine overdose.

Once a person is addicted to a drug such as cocaine, it is extremely hard to kick the habit. But it is possible. It's never too late. At the end of this book you will find a section on getting help if you or someone you know is addicted to cocaine. Remember, there's help if you need it. All you have to do is ask.

4 Cocaine, Your Nose, and the Rest of Your Body

Cocaine can actually be taken three different ways. It can be smoked, injected, or—the way it affects noses most directly—snorted.

SNORTING

When a person is going to snort cocaine, he or she breathes it into the nose in the form of a fine, smooth powder. The cocaine is then absorbed into the bloodstream through the soft tissues inside the nasal passages.

Because the "high" is short lived, the user snorts more and more cocaine, until the soft tissues inside the nose are swollen and numb. The more cocaine ingested, the more damage is done to these tissues.

Nose Damage

Cocaine is like a tornado, damaging everything in its path. Because cocaine acts as an anesthetic, the user doesn't usually feel much pain while snorting. In truth, however, as you snort more and more, your nose is getting severely damaged. Here are some of the painful—and pretty disgusting—things that happen to your nose when you use cocaine:

 First your nose feels stuffed up, as if you had a cold, and then it starts to run. This is because the cocaine seriously irritates your sinuses.

 After you snort cocaine several times, the inside of your nose will start to dry out. This makes it crack and bleed. You may also start to develop sores on your nose and upper lip.

Are you ready to be grossed out even more? In addicts who have used cocaine heavily, the drug actually starts to eat holes in the septum (the bone that separates your nostrils). Fixing these holes is going to take a lot more than a few Band-Aids. We're talking serious surgery here.

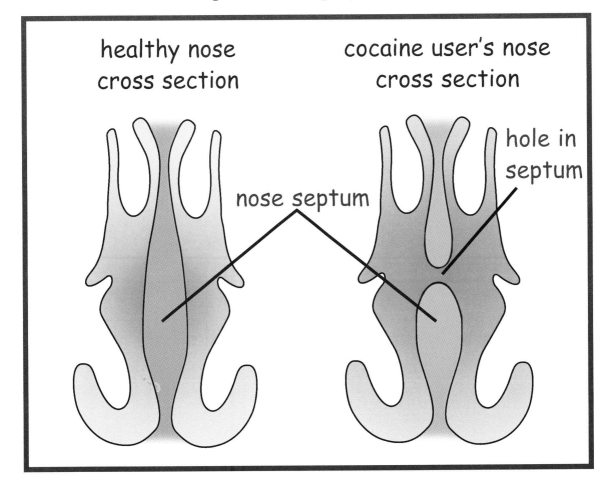

healthy nose cross section

cocaine user's nose cross section

nose septum

hole in septum

Another serious side effect of cocaine on the nose is that it can completely ruin your sense of smell. This happens because cocaine makes the blood vessels in your nose constrict, or get smaller. Over time, this prevents blood from reaching your nose. When that happens, your nerve cells—and eventually the flesh in your nose—actually die, making your nose pretty much a dead organ.

A less obvious but really serious risk of snorting cocaine is catching dangerous diseases like hepatitis or HIV, the virus that causes AIDS. How can that happen from snorting? Well, as you know, people use straws (or rolled up pieces of paper) to inhale cocaine powder into their nose. Often these straws are passed around from user to user. Since cocaine users often have bloody noses or cracked skin, it's very easy for some of their blood to get on the straw. If an infected user gets blood on the straw and then passes the straw to other users who have cracked skin or sores, the infections can enter those users' bodies and make them sick.

OTHER WAYS TO TAKE COCAINE

You have already learned about the dangers of snorting cocaine. You know that snorting cocaine can make you lose your sense of smell and give you nosebleeds and sores on your nose and top lip. It can also make it hard for you to swallow, it can make your voice hoarse, and it can mess

nose and lip sores

Infections, such as nose or lip sores, are often spread from one user to another through the sharing of cocaine straws.

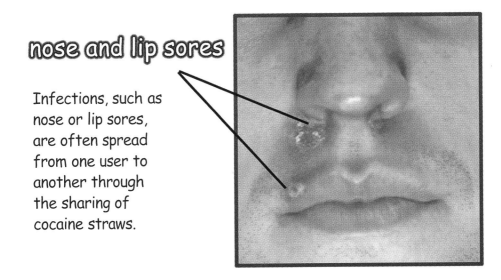

up your sinuses, giving you a stuffy, runny nose. On top of that, diseases can be passed from one user to the other if there is blood from an infected person on a shared straw used for snorting.

Smoking Cocaine

Do you know about the other ways of doing cocaine? One way is to smoke it. People smoke a form of cocaine called crack. Because crack is even stronger and purer than regular cocaine, it is more addictive. In fact, some researchers say that crack is actually the most addictive substance in the world.

Crack is also one of the most dangerous drugs around. Smoking crack can give you really terrible chest pain and breathing problems like wheezing and a cough that doesn't go away. Your lips, tongue, and throat will become extremely dry, and your voice will get hoarse.

Smoking crack can do other damage, too. It can singe your eyebrows and eyelashes, and even burn your skin. In 1980, actor and comedian Richard Pryor suffered mostly third-degree burns on more than half of his body from a bad accident while using crack.

The most dangerous thing smoking crack can do to you is make your lungs bleed. Bleeding lungs mean that oxygen from the air isn't being passed around your body the way it should be. This can lead to many prob-

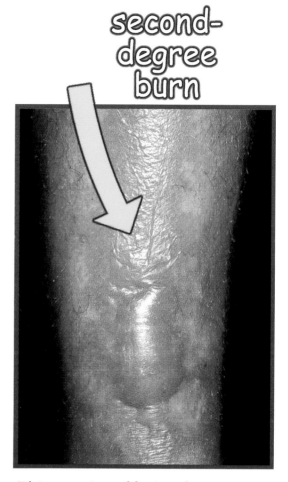

second-degree burn

This man is suffering from second-degree burns. This type of burn can result in shock so acute (severe) that the body's blood pressure will drop to a dangerously low level, possibly resulting in death.

lems in all parts of your body, including the heart, brain, kidneys, stomach, and liver.

Injecting Cocaine

The third way of doing cocaine is by injecting it into your veins with a needle. Injecting cocaine over and over again can scar your veins for life. In addition, if you inject anything into your veins enough times, your veins get so irritated and infected that they close up. When that happens, blood can't reach your arms, fingers, or wherever you have been injecting, and you eventually lose control of these body parts.

Injecting cocaine (or any drug) with dirty needles can lead to really bad infections in your heart and can also give you pneumonia, tuberculosis, and other diseases. One of the worst things that you can get from injecting cocaine is HIV, the virus that causes AIDS. You can also get hepatitis B and C, which are serious diseases that can lead to liver damage and other health problems.

The reason people get these diseases from injecting cocaine is that they share needles with people who already have the diseases. If infected blood—even the tiniest amount—stays on the needle, the disease can be passed to others who use it.

COCAINE AND YOUR BRAIN

Cocaine works on the part of your brain that makes you have strong feelings about things. People who use cocaine don't feel hungry or tired when they are high. Instead, they feel like they have a lot of strength, power, and energy. Sounds pretty good, doesn't it?

But cocaine also messes up the chemicals in your brain. By changing around these chemicals, cocaine makes you think that you want cocaine very badly and that it's a good and necessary thing.This feeling is called a craving. A craving is a very strong desire (want) for something. Have you ever really, really wanted chocolate or ice cream? Did you feel like you might just go nuts if you didn't get that food?

The craving probably went away after a while, either because you finally got the food or you were distracted by something else. Food cravings are normal and pretty harmless. But a cocaine craving can be dangerous because if you continue to satisfy the craving you may become addicted. When you are addicted to something, your body doesn't just want it badly anymore—now it needs that thing in order to just feel normal.

clogged vein

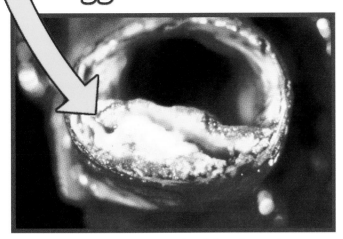

Cocaine use can cause the blood to clot abnormally fast, which can lead to a heart attack or stroke.

COCAINE AND YOUR HEART

Your heart is responsible for pumping blood that is full of oxygen to all areas of your body. If your heart can't do its job, your body doesn't get the oxygen it needs to survive, and you die. In general, cocaine makes your heart beat faster than it should. Cocaine can also cause your blood to clot much faster than it normally would. If a clot forms in one of the major passageways that carry blood to the heart, it can lead to a heart attack. This is why people who have never had any heart problems can die from a surprise heart attack, even after just one use of cocaine.

COCAINE AND THE REST OF YOUR BODY

Have you ever heard someone say something like "Your body is your temple"? Of course, this doesn't mean that your body is a kind of building. But like a temple, your body is sacred and should be treated with respect. You get only one body in your lifetime, and how you treat it and take care of it when you are young has a lot to do with how long it will last. Using cocaine can cause damage all over your body. Once these body parts are ruined, there's usually no repairing them. And your body can't function for long with damaged parts.

What are we trying to say here? Let's get to the point. These are the facts: Cocaine can harm your heart, brain, blood vessels, lungs, throat, and, of course, your nose. If any one of these systems becomes too damaged, you will die.

WITHDRAWAL

If someone who is addicted to cocaine suddenly stops using the drug, he or she will experience withdrawal, or "coming down." This is a very painful process that happens with many different drugs.

The happy feeling that the cocaine caused at first goes away and the person ends up feeling really, really sick. People going through withdrawal often feel hungry, irritable (crabby), apathetic (not caring what happens), depressed (very down and blue), and paranoid (worried that everyone is out to get them).

That's not all. Users in withdrawal have intense crav-ings, think a lot about committing suicide, lose interest in sex, and suffer from serious sleeping problems like insomnia (not being able to sleep) or sleeping too much. They also probably have some stomach problems like diarrhea or constipation.

One of the scariest symptoms of cocaine withdrawal is hallucinations. When you hallucinate, you think you see or hear something that isn't really there. People in cocaine withdrawal may imagine that there are snakes, worms, or bugs crawling on their bodies. They may even believe they can feel these creepy crawlies on their skin.

Some withdrawal symptoms last for only a few days. Others can stick around for months. The worst part of withdrawal is that lots of times users don't have anyone to help them get through the painful process and they lose the willpower to quit drugs. Instead of sticking it out, they start taking cocaine again to make the bad feelings of withdrawal go away.

After you use cocaine regularly for a while, it really gets into your system and starts to damage things all over your body. Here are some bad effects of using cocaine: headaches, blurry or fuzzy vision, seeing spots, coughing, breathing problems, seizures, lung damage, overdose, and death.

$$COCAINE AND YOUR CASH$$

Some people say that cocaine users "snort all their money away" or that "all of their money goes right up their nose." As weird as those phrases may sound, they're pretty accurate. Buying enough cocaine to satisfy an addiction can cost you from hundreds to thousands of dollars every week. Spending all your money on cocaine will leave you broke and maybe even homeless.

5 Keeping Clean

As one of the main entrances to your respiratory system—the system in charge of the all-important job of breathing to keep you alive—your nose is a vital part of your body that must be kept healthy. Becoming addicted to cocaine is the easy part—most of the time it happens before you even know it. Beating the addiction may be the hardest thing you ever do, but thousands of people do it every year.

There are many organizations out there that want to help addicts get over their drug habit. For information and support, contact some of the sources listed in the back of this book.

GETTING HELP

For many people who are addicted to cocaine, the hardest part of getting over the addiction is admitting that they have a problem in the first place. Some people are too proud to admit it, and other people are just too embarrassed. But the fact is, if you don't admit your problem and you don't get help, cocaine will mess up your nose, the rest of your body, and eventually your whole life.

For those of you who are reading this book because you think someone you know may have a problem with cocaine, you may be able to save that person's life by sharing this information with him or her. It can be very difficult to talk to someone about a drug problem, but it doesn't pay to be shy when it comes to the dangers of drugs. Contact the places listed in this book for advice about how to protect yourself and those around you.

GLOSSARY

addiction   The physical and/or psychological need for a drug in order to get through each day and feel normal.

anesthetic   A painkilling drug that causes loss of feeling or consciousness.

cartilage   Elastic tissue that makes up the long part of the nose (along with bone) and connects the nose to the skull.

craving   An intense and urgent need for a drug.

pharynx   The throat.

respiration   The process of breathing in oxygen and breathing out carbon dioxide.

respiratory system   The set of organs, including the nose, mouth, and lungs, that enable you to breathe.

seizure   A sudden attack or convulsion, usually due to a physical disorder or to drug use.

septum   A wall made of cartilage and bone that divides the nose.

FOR MORE INFORMATION

Hotlines

Boy's Town National Hotline
(800) 448-3000

National Drug and Alcohol
Treatment Referral Service
(800) 662-HELP [662-4357]

National Substance Abuse Hotline
(800) DRUG HELP [378-4437]
(800) HELP 111 [435-7111]

Youth Crisis Hotline
(800) HIT HOME [448-4663]

Organizations

National Clearinghouse for
Alcohol and Drug
Information
P.O. Box 2345
Rockville, MD 20847-2345
(301) 468-2600
Web site: http://www.health.org

National Council on Alcoholism
and Drug Dependence
12 West 21st Street, 7th Floor
New York, NY 10010
(800) NCA-CALL [622-2255]
Web site: http://www.hcadd.org

Students Against Drugs and
Alcohol (SADA)
7443 E. 68th Street
Tulsa, OK 74133
(918) 249-1315
e-mail: sada@sada.org

Web Sites

DARE
http://www.sayno.com

Go Ask Alice
http://www.goaskalice.columbia.edu

Web of Addictions
http://www.well.com/user/woa

FOR FURTHER READING

Glass, George. *Drugs and Fitting In*. New York: Rosen Publishing Group, 1998.

Gutman, Bill. *Harmful to Your Health*. New York: Twenty-First Century Books, 1996.

Nagle, Jeanne M. *Drug Addiction*. New York: Rosen Publishing Group, 1999.

Phillips, Lynn. *Life Issues: Drug Abuse*. New York: Marshall Cavendish, 1994.

Robbins, Paul R. *Crack and Cocaine Drug Dangers*. Springfield, NJ: Enslow Publishers, 1999.

Ryan, Elizabeth A. *Straight Talk About Drugs and Alcohol*. New York: Facts on File, 1995.

Shulman, Jeffrey. *Focus on Cocaine and Crack*. New York: Twenty-First Century Books, 1995.

Smith-McLaughlin, Miriam, and Sandra Peyser-Hazouri. *Addiction: The High That Brings You Down*. Springfield, NJ: Enslow Publishers, 1997.

Turck, Mary C. *Crack and Cocaine*. Parsippany, NJ: Silver Burdett Press, 1999.

INDEX

B

Belushi, John, 29
blood clots, 38
brain, 5, 10, 11, 17, 18, 36, 37

C

cilia, 16, 17
Coca-Cola, 28
cocaine
    addiction and, 24–29, 34, 37
    as an anesthetic, 26, 31
    damaging effects of, 5, 19, 21,
        24–28, 31–41
    diseases and, 32–33, 35
    doctors and, 27, 28
    heart attacks and, 5, 21, 38
    history of, 25–28
    illegality of, 21–22, 23, 24, 28
    kicking the habit of, 29, 39–41
    medicines and, 27, 28
    money and, 25, 27, 28, 41
    reasons people use, 20, 25, 26,
        27, 28, 37
    teens and, 4, 20–21
    withdrawal from, 39–41
coca plant, 25–26
crack cocaine, 34–35
craving, 37

I

infection, 11, 33–34
injecting cocaine, 30, 36
    sharing needles while, 36

L

limbic system, 18
lungs, 6, 8, 10, 12, 15, 35, 39

N

nares, 9
nasal cavity, 9–10, 15
nose, 5, 6–11

P

Pryor, Richard, 35
Pure Food and Drug Act of 1906, 28

R

respiratory system, 6, 8–14, 34–35, 42

S

sense of smell, 8, 14–17, 18, 32–33
septum, 7, 9, 32
smoking cocaine, 30, 34–35
    burns and, 35
sneezing, 16
snorting cocaine, 19, 30–33
stimulants, 24

CREDITS

About the Author

Melanie Ann Apel is a pediatric respiratory therapist at Children's Memorial Hospital in Chicago. She has a degree in respiratory care from National-Louis University and a degree in theater arts from Bradley University. Her other books for Rosen include *Drug Interactions,* as well as twelve titles in the PowerKids Press *Let's Talk About . . .* series. When she is not writing, Melanie likes to figure skate, travel, and spend time with loved ones.

Acknowledgments

The author wishes to thank Mindy Apel for her research assistance.

Photo Credits

Design and Layout

Laura Murawski